Analysis of Performance for GCSE PE

Teacher Guide

Julie Walmsley

© 2004 Folens Limited, on behalf of the author.

UK: Folens Publishers, Apex Business Centre, Boscombe Road, Dunstable, LU5 4RL.
Email: folens@folens.com

Ireland: Folens Publishers, Greenhills Road, Tallaght, Dublin 24.
Email: info@folens.ie

Poland: JUKA, ul. Renesansowa 38, Warsaw 01-905.

Editor: Geoff Tuttle
Layout artist: Suzanne Ward
Illustrations: Catherine Ward
Cover design: Martin Cross
Cover image: © Jon Feingersh/CORBIS

First published 2004 by Folens Limited.

Every effort has been made to contact copyright holders of material used in this publication. If any copyright holder has been overlooked, we should be pleased to make any necessary arrangements.
British Library Cataloguing in Publication Data. A catalogue record for this publication is available from the British Library.

ISBN 1-84303-630-4

Analysis of Performance for GCSE PE – Teacher Guide
© Folens

Contents

Introduction to the teacher guide

Information to the teacher

The teacher's pack aims to provide the back up needed to use the analysis booklet and adapt the contents to other activities. It will explain how the work matches up with boards' requirements linking them with examples of tables, forms and check-off lists for the pupils to use in lesson time.

The pack is divided into the following sections:

1 Information for teachers
2 Understanding the analysis forms
3 Practical applications
4 Officiating
5 Feedback
6 Blank templates forms

By making these divisions the user can locate the most appropriate section needed at the time. The areas covered not only include how to analyse performance but also details of ways of applying training principles, methods and practices to an activity, the demands of officiating and ways of giving feedback. Together the different sections complete a package of related information giving the pupils the best chance of success and the teacher ready-made sheets for use in class. The aim is to make the analysis of performance section of the syllabus as straightforward as possible.

The book provides concrete examples of how to set out work and what to include for a good answer. The activity examples used are athletics, football and netball. The reason for this is that they are often popular options with candidates.

Feedback

There are a variety of suggestions of ways to gather information on and conduct a feedback session. Ideas of what to ask, how to record and ways to encourage the performer to add to the feedback are provided.

Blank forms

The book provides forms already completed for the three examples used – athletics, football and netball. There are also blank forms that can be adapted to other activities. Pupils can be guided as to how the forms can be customised for their chosen activity.

The blank sheets can be used in class and will provide a record of the work covered. The accumulation of these will build up as a portfolio of the pupils' efforts. They can be marked and referred to throughout the course so improvements can be made in readiness for the final examination.

A note on stretching

The issue of stretching is one that has caused much debate among teachers and coaches. In the pupil book we have chosen to include a mixture of both dynamic and static stretches. Static stretching has been considered the safest and most effective means of preparing for and recovering from exercise. It involves gently moving into a position and holding it for several seconds. Dynamic (ballistic) stretching involves performers moving in and out of stretches, sometimes appearing to bounce into them. Traditionally this type of stretching was considered less effective and was believed to cause injuries such as microscopic muscle tears and damage to growth plates in younger children. All the same, it is increasingly used, particularly by older and more experienced performers, and needs good levels of coordination, skill and understanding to be done well. However, it is vital that performers should not move on to this type of stretching until muscles have first been warmed up using static stretching.

AQA Specification

The information in the analysis book covers several areas for AQA. These concentrate on:

Skill area C – *Understanding, Observing and Applying Rules and Conventions*

Skill area D – *Analyse and take action to improve their own and others' performance*

Skill area E – *Adopting different roles in the activity*

The book will cover all of these skill areas. It aims to give a complete bank of information necessary for the pupils to be fully informed for these parts of the syllabus and consequently provide the best chance for success.

Skill area C – *Understanding, Observing and Applying Rules and Conventions*

Both general concepts and specific information about rules and regulations of the chosen activity examples is provided about officiating. The pupil will be required to combine their knowledge of the rules, tactics and experience of the game in an officiating capacity. The information aims to familiarise the pupil with some specific terminology, official signals and the areas an official should concentrate on to be efficient and effective.

Skill area D – *Analyse and take action to improve their own and others' performance*

This area requires the pupil to identify strengths and weaknesses of a performance. In order to do this the pupils must gain information and develop an understanding of the activity. Three sporting examples are used in the book, providing a starting point for when the candidates work on the analysis of their own chosen activity.

An analysis form has been especially designed for AQA to cover all the specification requirements. It shows what areas need to be covered in the analysis process in order to give a full answer whilst encouraging the use of technical terminology. The forms can easily be kept and produced as evidence of the work in the final examination.

Skill area E – *Adopting different roles in the activity*

The candidate should gain experience and competence in officiating an activity. By showing some of the different roles in an activity, pupils will understand the job each has to play in the overall performance. Comparing different managerial styles will provide an understanding of the varied ways success can be achieved. Pointing out the components of each style will hopefully provide the pupils with some possible options that suit their personality and they will be able to blend them into their own leadership technique.

Edexcel Specification

The Edexcel analysis of performance matrix

The syllabus is set out with five areas; each have a mark weighting linked with them.

This is how the book meets the demands of the sections:

- Rules, regulations and terminology
- Observation and analysis
- Evaluation
- Planning stragegies, tactics, practices and training to improve performance
- Understanding the principles and roles of leadership to improve performance

Rules, regulations and terminology

A general comment is made on how rules, regulations and terminology play their part in activities. An appreciation of how rules keep the game safe, individual and fair is provided at the beginning of the book.

Section 4 is devoted to the officiating of each of the example activities. Specific hand signals, terminology and duties of the activities are set out.

Observation and analysis

The book aims to show what to look for in a performance. It suggests what makes up a good performance and clearly sets these ideas out. Ways are given of how an analysis may take shape. Examples include the way observations can be marked against a given criteria or a record of the number of times skills are attempted. There are several suggestions of how feedback may be relayed to the performer; giving the pupil the opportunity to choose the one that most fits their style/personality/ability.

Evaluation

The activity examples chosen identify areas of both weakness and strength. An analysis form has been especially designed to cover all the specification requirements. It clearly sets out the areas for a full answer and also provides a means of keeping evidence of work for the final examination. Pupils can, by using the model, give a detailed evaluation of a performance. They will be asked to compare observed performance with the perfect model. Understanding the components of a top class performance will make it easier to analyse that of a less experienced performer.

Planning strategies, tactics, practices and training to improve performance

There are suggested practices and training methods linked with the performance examples and how they can be used in a PEP (Personal Exercise Programme). By using these as a model, pupils can devise their own PEP for their chosen area.

The area of planning complex strategies and the explanation of tactics I have left to the practical sessions of the GCSE course. The practical experience in the game situation will provide the understanding of the need for and changes to tactical development required for success in the activity.

Understanding the principles and roles of leadership to improve performance

By showing the different roles in an activity pupils will see the job each has to play in the overall performance. Comparing different leadership styles will provide an understanding of the varied ways success can be achieved. Pointing out the components of each style will hopefully provide the pupils with some possible options that suit their personality to blend into their own leadership technique.

OCR Specification

OCR analysis assessment covers three areas:

- Recognition of strengths and weaknesses in own and others' performance

- Apply knowledge of methods, practices and techniques to improve performance

- Officiate/referee in a game/competition

Recognition of strengths and weaknesses in own and others' performance

The book provides information on what to look for in a good performance and sets these ideas out clearly. Different examples are given of ways of analysing so the pupils can choose the method that suits them.

The specially designed analysis sheet for OCR sets out, on one double-sided page, the board's requirements for the successful studying of a performance. The form clearly follows the board's specification guiding the pupil to a full answer. The analysis sheet can be adapted to any activity. All pupils will be able to use the form both for practice and final attempts. Gaining familiarity with the form will make it easier for the pupil to use and the teacher to mark.

Apply knowledge of methods, practices and techniques to improve performance

The book uses three activities to show the pupils how the training principles, methods and practices can be adapted to them. These can be used as a guide to the candidates when working on their own activity.

The analysis sheet further develops the process by providing space for the pupils to combine their knowledge of the activity with training principles, methods and practices to improve performance.

Officiate/referee in a game/competition

A general comment on how rules, regulations and terminology play their part in activities is explained. Section 4 is devoted to the officiating of each of the example activities. Specific hand signals, terminology and duties of the officials are set out.

The pupils will be required to apply the information to their chosen activity. They will be expected to combine their own knowledge of the rules, tactics and personal experience in an officiating capacity.

Pointing the pupils in the right direction

The book works through the issues for completing work on athletics, football and netball.

Each are set out in the same way showing that each activity deserves equal treatment. This also has the secondary benefit of making the teacher's job easier when dealing with a variety of activities as the guides given are common to all.

Within the text are suggestions to the pupils of what their course of action may be and where the focus of their energies should be directed. Some of the information will come from their own knowledge of the sport but they must support this and make sure of the facts. To make a more in depth response they should refer to coaching publications. The teacher's knowledge will help to direct them to websites, coaching manuals, videos and CD Roms.

Each example activity section has the same suggestions pointing the pupils in the right direction:

- Know what makes up your chosen sport

- Be able to identify the perfect model

- Know how the action is made up of small parts

- Know the building blocks for the action

- Adapt a warm-up to your chosen sport

- Remember an appropriate cool down to avoid possible discomfort

- Gather as much information about your sport from different sources

- Apply your knowledge of the principles of training

- Adapt the most appropriate training methods to your chosen sport

- Apply your knowledge of training practices to your chosen sport

     Analysis of Performance for GCSE PE – Teacher Guide

Understanding the AQA analysis form (side 1)

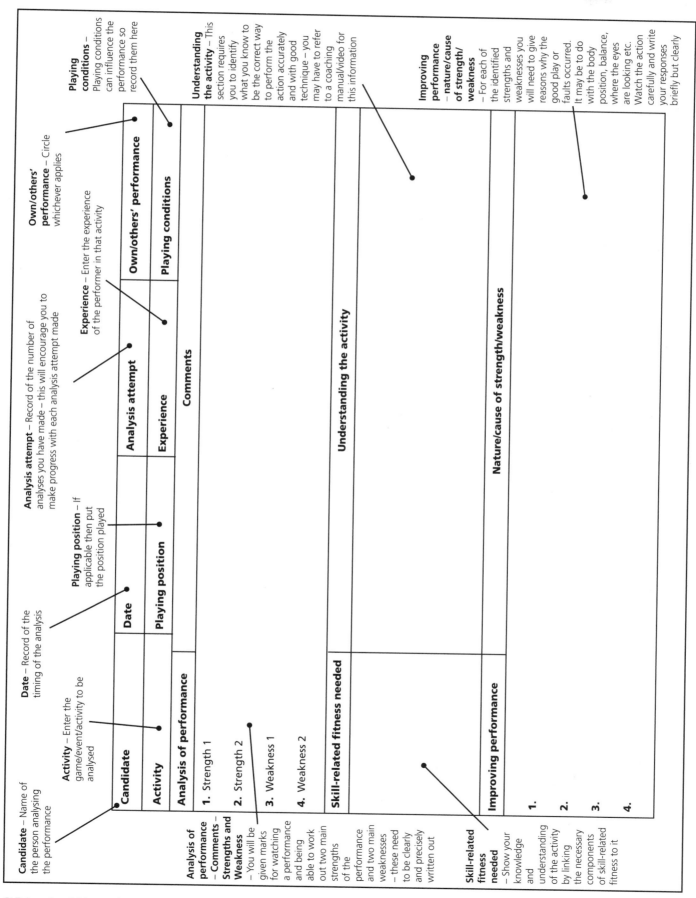

Understanding the AQA analysis form (side 2)

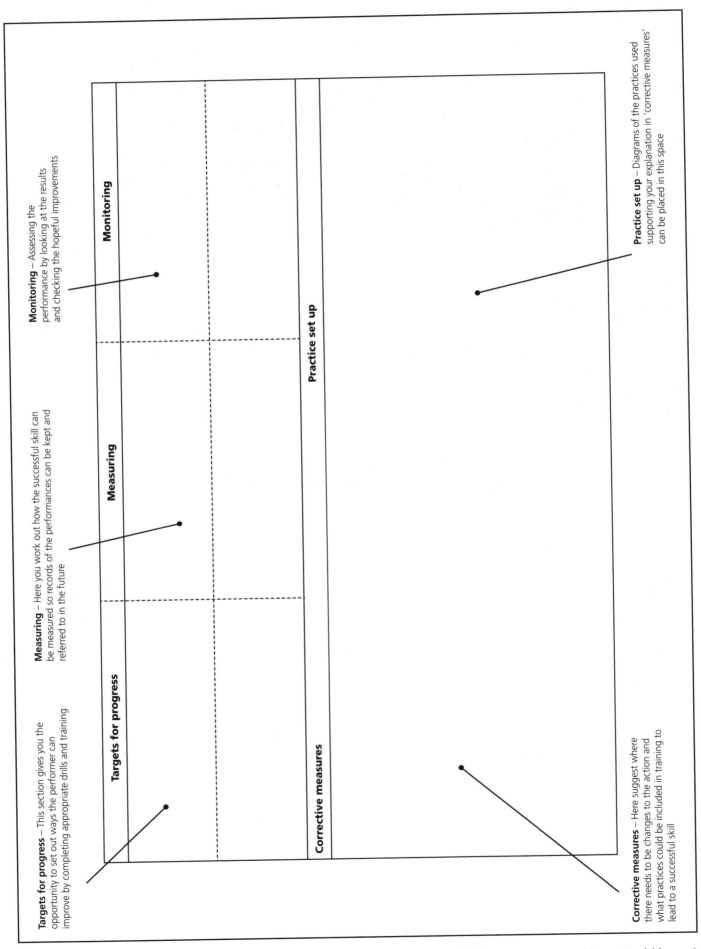

Monitoring – Assessing the performance by looking at the results and checking the hopeful improvements

Monitoring

Measuring – Here you work out how the successful skill can be measured so records of the performances can be kept and referred to in the future

Measuring

Practice set up

Practice set up – Diagrams of the practices used supporting your explanation in 'corrective measures' can be placed in this space

Targets for progress – This section gives you the opportunity to set out ways the performer can improve by completing appropriate drills and training

Targets for progress

Corrective measures

Corrective measures – Here suggest where there needs to be changes to the action and what practices could be included in training to lead to a successful skill

Analysis of Performance for GCSE PE – Teacher Guide

Understanding the Edexcel analysis form (side 1)

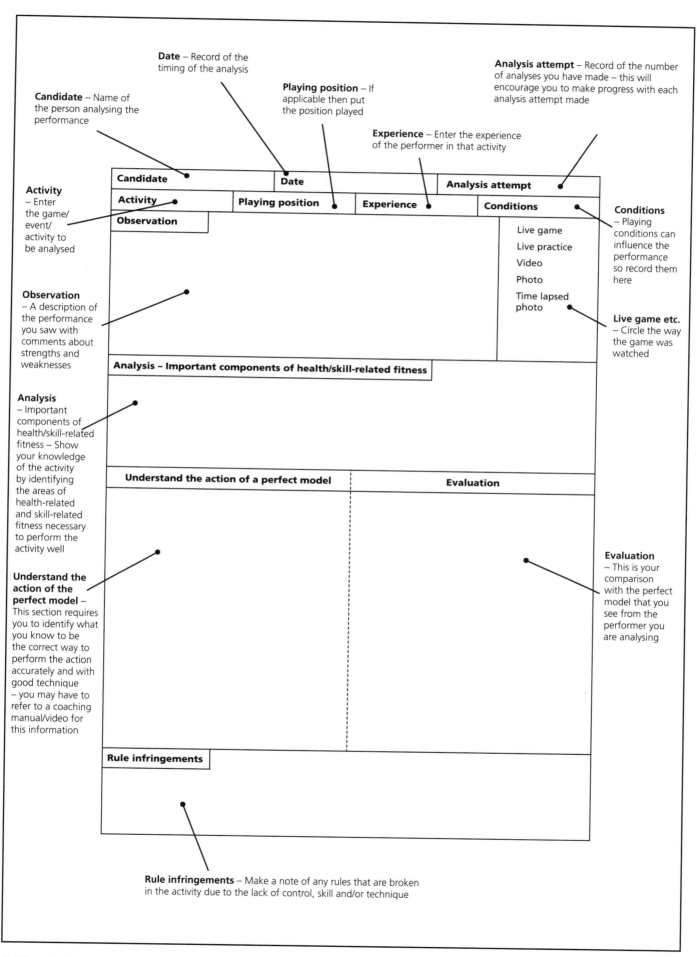

Date – Record of the timing of the analysis

Playing position – If applicable then put the position played

Analysis attempt – Record of the number of analyses you have made – this will encourage you to make progress with each analysis attempt made

Candidate – Name of the person analysing the performance

Experience – Enter the experience of the performer in that activity

Activity – Enter the game/ event/ activity to be analysed

Conditions – Playing conditions can influence the performance so record them here

Observation – A description of the performance you saw with comments about strengths and weaknesses

Live game etc. – Circle the way the game was watched

Analysis – Important components of health/skill-related fitness – Show your knowledge of the activity by identifying the areas of health-related and skill-related fitness necessary to perform the activity well

Understand the action of the perfect model – This section requires you to identify what you know to be the correct way to perform the action accurately and with good technique – you may have to refer to a coaching manual/video for this information

Evaluation – This is your comparison with the perfect model that you see from the performer you are analysing

Rule infringements – Make a note of any rules that are broken in the activity due to the lack of control, skill and/or technique

Candidate	Date	Analysis attempt
Activity	Playing position	Experience	Conditions

Observation

Conditions:
Live game
Live practice
Video
Photo
Time lapsed photo

Analysis – Important components of health/skill-related fitness

Understand the action of a perfect model	Evaluation

Rule infringements

Understanding the Edexcel analysis form (side 2)

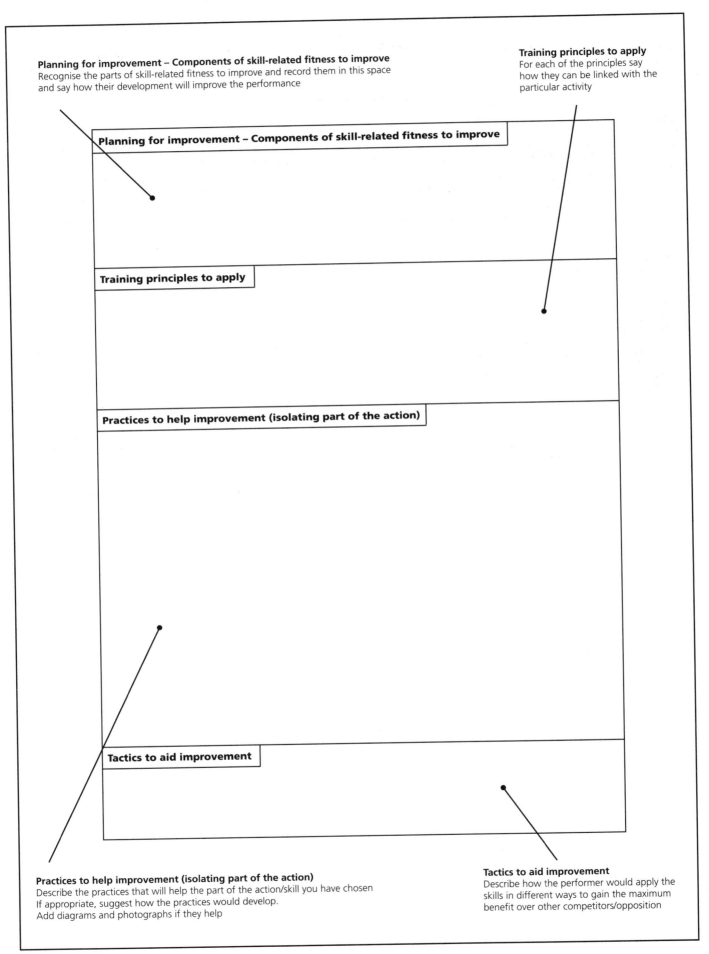

Planning for improvement – Components of skill-related fitness to improve
Recognise the parts of skill-related fitness to improve and record them in this space and say how their development will improve the performance

Training principles to apply
For each of the principles say how they can be linked with the particular activity

Planning for improvement – Components of skill-related fitness to improve

Training principles to apply

Practices to help improvement (isolating part of the action)

Tactics to aid improvement

Practices to help improvement (isolating part of the action)
Describe the practices that will help the part of the action/skill you have chosen
If appropriate, suggest how the practices would develop.
Add diagrams and photographs if they help

Tactics to aid improvement
Describe how the performer would apply the skills in different ways to gain the maximum benefit over other competitors/opposition

Understanding the OCR analysis form (side 1)

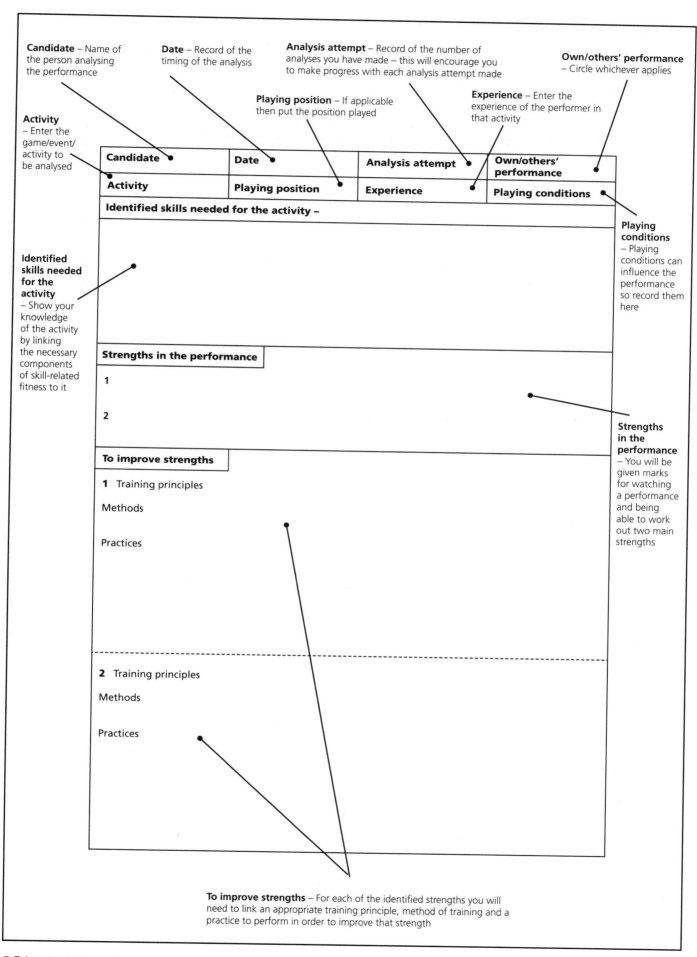

Candidate – Name of the person analysing the performance

Date – Record of the timing of the analysis

Analysis attempt – Record of the number of analyses you have made – this will encourage you to make progress with each analysis attempt made

Own/others' performance – Circle whichever applies

Playing position – If applicable then put the position played

Experience – Enter the experience of the performer in that activity

Activity – Enter the game/event/activity to be analysed

Candidate	Date	Analysis attempt	Own/others' performance
Activity	Playing position	Experience	Playing conditions

Identified skills needed for the activity –

Identified skills needed for the activity – Show your knowledge of the activity by linking the necessary components of skill-related fitness to it

Playing conditions – Playing conditions can influence the performance so record them here

Strengths in the performance

1

2

Strengths in the performance – You will be given marks for watching a performance and being able to work out two main strengths

To improve strengths

1 Training principles

Methods

Practices

2 Training principles

Methods

Practices

To improve strengths – For each of the identified strengths you will need to link an appropriate training principle, method of training and a practice to perform in order to improve that strength

Understanding the OCR analysis form (side 2)

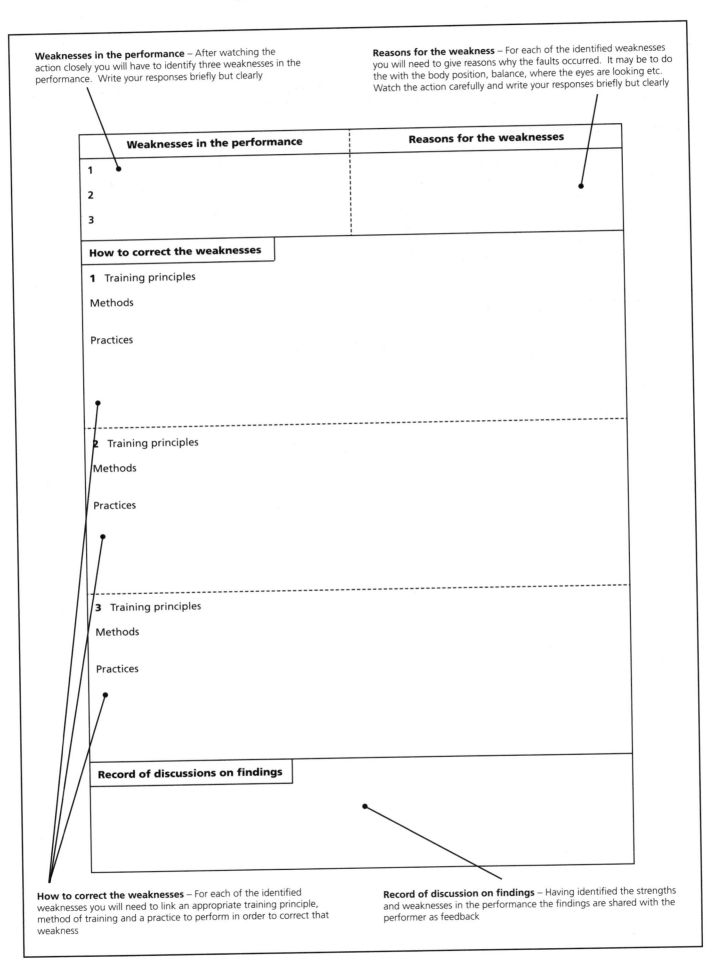

Weaknesses in the performance – After watching the action closely you will have to identify three weaknesses in the performance. Write your responses briefly but clearly

Reasons for the weakness – For each of the identified weaknesses you will need to give reasons why the faults occurred. It may be to do the with the body position, balance, where the eyes are looking etc. Watch the action carefully and write your responses briefly but clearly

Weaknesses in the performance	Reasons for the weaknesses
1	
2	
3	

How to correct the weaknesses

1 Training principles

Methods

Practices

2 Training principles

Methods

Practices

3 Training principles

Methods

Practices

Record of discussions on findings

How to correct the weaknesses – For each of the identified weaknesses you will need to link an appropriate training principle, method of training and a practice to perform in order to correct that weakness

Record of discussion on findings – Having identified the strengths and weaknesses in the performance the findings are shared with the performer as feedback

Analysis of Performance for GCSE PE – Teacher Guide

Training

Whatever the activity, recording the training and the exercise completed will be evidence of the effort made. It will give the pupil ownership of their training and they will be able to refer to it when they need to.

Having a training diary or record sheet can:

- Focus the performer on the tasks/exercises
- Guide the performer to the frequency, intensity, time and type of exercises to perform (AQA – FID – frequency, intensity, duration)
- Set out the targets and may as a result motivate the performer
- The record can be compared with future training programmes
- Visualise the progress made by physically showing them how far they are into the training
- Will show and remind them of the effort made

Testing and measuring

It should be emphasised that for a successful training programme to be devised the performer should be tested in the areas pertinent to their chosen activity.

Possible areas to be tested:

- Endurance
- Flexibility
- Strength
- Agility
- Speed
- Power

Training principles

The exercises used should be relevant to the sport and be able to improve the skills or parts of skills for that activity. SPORT (Specificity, Progression, Overload, Reversibility and Tedium) should be applied to all training programmes.

Training methods

The choice of training methods will depend on their suitability and adaptability to the sport and the performer's preferences. There also may be a reason to add variety to the work in order to keep the interest of the performer.

Possible training methods to use:

- Circuit training
- Weight training
- Fartlek training
- Interval training

By correctly combining all of the areas set out in this section, there is a strong likelihood that an appropriate training programme will be successfully devised.

RECORD OF COMPLETED TESTING AND EXERCISE SESSIONS

WEEK 1

Name		Date		Activity training for	
Test results					
ENDURANCE	FLEXIBILITY	ARM STRENGTH	AGILITY	SPEED	POWER
BLEEP TEST	SIT AND REACH	PRESS-UPS	ILLINOIS RUN	SHUTTLES	VERTICAL JUMP

TRAINING SESSIONS TO COMPLETE *(Tick box if completed)*

WEEK 2

CIRCUIT TRAINING	☐	WEIGHT TRAINING	☐	SKILLS TRAINING	☐	GAME PRACTICE	☐
Comments							

WEEK 3

	☐		☐		☐		☐

WEEK 4

	☐		☐		☐		☐

WEEK 5

	☐		☐		☐		☐

WEEK 6

RETEST RESULTS

	ENDURANCE	FLEXIBILITY	ARM STRENGTH	AGILITY	SPEED	POWER
RESULT						
CHANGE						

Analysis of Performance for GCSE PE – Teacher Guide

Exercises to improve specific areas – Speed

The nature of the activity dictates which skills it is necessary to develop. The demands of the activity require different physical development from the performer in order to be successful. It may be that each of the skill-related fitness components is required to perform the activity. Some, however, may have a varying degree of importance and so success relies on their development to an appropriate level. A number of activities need the performer to develop only a few of the components to succeed. These skills components should be identified early on in planning the training programme and work should concentrate on these.

Speed

There are many occasions when speed is necessary. When the shot putter makes an attempt then power is required. Power can, in simple terms, be called fast strength. A games player will need to move off the spot quickly and decisively to mark or escape an opponent. The player can use the following to develop their ability to perform short bursts of sprinting – shuttle runs and short maximal runs over short distances (20 metres).

Shuttle runs are a way of increasing speed over a short distance.

Quick footwork of football players will also enable them to run, dribble and dodge the opponent at speed, practices for this include – step ups, bench astride, side shuffles and quick stepping on a line.

Side shuffles speed up the movement of the feet.

Throwing games sometimes require the ball to remain in the hands for as short a time as possible so the time the ball is received and passed has to be short. Practices to develop hand speed are – catch and throw exercises and batting the ball with palms to a wall.

Catch and throw exercises performed at maximum pace quicken the throwing action.

Exercises to improve specific areas – Conditioning

Conditioning can be adapted to events requiring explosive strength. Plyometrics, specific exercises and medicine ball work can be part of a conditioning programme.

Plyometrics is a training method used to improve explosive power needed in events such as shot put. It can involve jumping, bounding and hopping exercises. In order to improve explosive strength, the rate at which the exercises are performed is crucial.

The effect of plyometrics is an explosive body action, which can be seen by powerful muscular contractions as a result of quick lengthening of the muscles involved. Examples of these exercises are tuck jumps, jumps from standing, drop and hold drills, press-ups and claps, bunny hops for distance, double jumps up stairs/over small hurdles.

Plyometric exercise example – Double jumps up stairs.

Specific exercises work a particular part of the body in a certain way. Examples of these exercises are single leg squats, single leg squat hops, skipping or bouncing on the toes, astride jumps onto a bench, sideways hopping over a 15 cm hurdle.

Specific exercise example – Single leg squats.

Medicine ball work uses the resistance of the ball and speed of the action to develop power There are different weights of medicine ball. Boys should use one 3 kg and girls 2 kg.

A conditioning programme can develop like any other increasing the frequency, intensity, time (duration) and type of exercise as the performer improves. Examples of exercises are single arm throw, chest passing and lay back double arm throw.

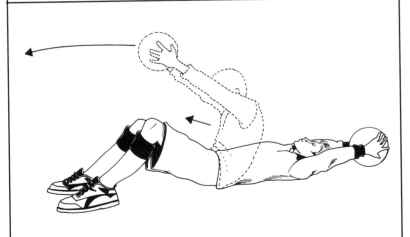

Medicine ball example – Lay back double arm throw.

Analysis of Performance for GCSE PE – Teacher Guide

Exercises to improve specific areas – Agility

Agility is important to performers needing to change direction quickly whilst still keeping balanced. The rigours of a team game or racket sport require much agility from the players when they try to dodge or mark an opponent or move to return an opponent's shot.

There are several drills designed to develop agility. Some can be adapted to different sports, some are sport specific. In rugby the player with the ball needs agility to dodge an opponent, the training exercises are very specific to the sport.

Exercises designed to develop agility include skipping running style, zigzag runs, tyre running, compass run and 'T' drills.

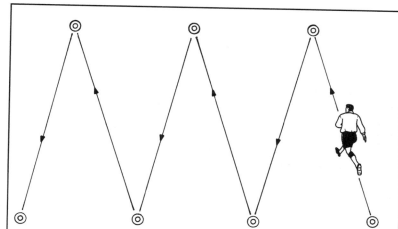

Zigzag runs demand quick feet and efficient changing of direction.

Agility relies on quick feet and controlling the centre of gravity as the body changes direction. The exercise drills should work the performer in the same way needed in the activity, copying the directions of movement and speed required.

Note: The performer should always face the same direction, therefore running forwards, sidewards and backwards.

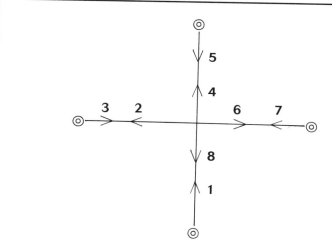

Compass runs work the performer in different directions.

Dribbling around cones is a simple drill combining the specific skill of close control and agility. This can be adapted to games where travelling with the ball is an essential skill of the game – football, hockey and basketball for instance.

Dribbling combines skill with agility.

Check-off list for athletics – shot put

Identifying skills

A coach will watch the performance and be able to identify its strengths and weaknesses. From these observations they will work out the best plan to enhance the strengths and either improve or eliminate the weaknesses. Sometimes changing the tactics will help to hide the weaknesses by reducing the situations where the skills are needed. A football player with a weak left foot may be positioned on the right side of the pitch so kicking with the left foot is required less frequently.

Check-off list for athletics – shot put

When analysing the action be mindful of the different phases making up the whole action. The performer should remember that the throw is the combination of force starting from the slower stronger muscles of the legs and pelvis to the faster but weaker muscles of the shoulders and arms. The following breaks down the action for the shift style of putting:

ANALYSIS SHEET FOR ATHLETICS – SHOT PUT		Tick if successful
GRIP	Shot at base of three, outspread fingers with thumb and little finger supporting	
STANCE	Shot in contact with the neck and elbow high.	
CROUCH	Facing the back of the circle	
	Weight on right leg	
	Body low and closed	
	Left knee in close to the right.	
SHIFT	Lean body towards the toe board	
	Drive back on right leg whilst extending left leg vigorously	
	Keeping body low	
	Rotate the hips outwards so at right angles with the closed shoulders.	
PUT POSITION	Weight transfers from back to front leg	
	Fast right pushing hips to the front	
	Right leg extends (causing the lift).	
LIFT	Left arm swings down and back	
	Right shoulder driven outwards.	
STRIKE	When shoulders square – with elbow high	
	Arm punches the shot out at the last moment as a result of the leg and hip action	
	Left shoulder kept high too.	
RELEASE	Approximately 40 degrees (elite athletes release between 30–40 degrees)	
	With elbow high and on line with the shot	
	Arm punches forward	
	Wrist flips so thumb pointing downwards.	
RECOVERY	Once shot released right leg moves to the front to stop forward motion.	

Check-off list for football – the long pass

The long pass is a ball played over about 25m. A defender, midfielder, winger or player taking the corners would use this pass in a game. Performing a successful long pass relies on combining accuracy, balance and coordination with power. Apart from the chip it is the only skill that lofts the ball into the air with any power. In the game the added dimension for success is the team-mate's readiness and anticipation of the pass.

ANALYSIS SHEET FOR FOOTBALL – LONG PASS		Tick if successful
APPROACH	Collect the ball or push it into a space from where it is best to kick.	
	Run from the side to approach the ball.	
BASE	Position the instep of the standing foot just behind the ball.	
	Weight of the body over the base for stability.	
PREPARATION	Kicking leg swings back.	
	Standing leg flexes.	
	Arm on the non-kicking side out to help balance the body.	
HEAD POSITION	Head up with eyes looking at the ball.	
BODY POSITION	Torso is kept upright and leaning slightly back.	
CONTACT	With the instep of the kicking foot.	
FOLLOW THROUGH	Kicking leg sweeps through beyond the ball.	
RECOVERY	Balance and stance recovered quickly in order to reposition on the field according to the outcome of the pass.	

Check-off list for netball – the plain shot

The plain shot is the most basic shot played. Although it is uncomplicated it does rely on balance, coordination, concentration and accuracy – just like all shots. Once this basic skill is mastered, variations can be applied developing the shooting skill.

It can be used anywhere in the circle and careful placement of the shooter's feet can keep the defender as far away as possible giving more chance of success. Once the shot has been played, direct and purposeful movement enables the shooter to take a rebound or make the defender's job more difficult.

The shooters can work together in the circle passing between each other until the optimum place for taking the shot is established by one of the players. The shooters can disguise a pass as a shot to take the opposition by surprise to gain a better space.

ANALYSIS SHEET FOR NETBALL – PLAIN SHOT		Tick if successful
BASE	Feet apart.	
	Weight evenly distributed.	
	Landing foot forward.	
SUPPORT OF BALL	Ball held above head.	
	Fingers spread, behind and underneath the ball.	
	Wrist cocked.	
	Other hand stabilising to the side. The shooting arm's elbow at right angles.	
AIMING	Head/hand/ball and target in line.	
	Eyes focusing on furthest point of ring.	
PREPARATION	Knees flexed then	
	Extend up through body ending with	
RELEASE	Extension of arm.	
	Ball directed up and away from body with	
	A snap of the wrist ('wave goodbye to the ball') – this applies back-spin to ball.	
FOLLOW THROUGH	In direction of goal.	
	Moving the feet towards the direction of the shot.	
	Avoid contact with defender.	

Analysis of Performance for GCSE PE – Teacher Guide

Analysis of the Officials – Athletics – Shot put judge

In full competitions there are a series of officials who conduct the organisation of the field events. There are usually different people to check the whole field area, the correct equipment is there, the competitors are in the right place, the performance is legal, measuring the attempt and checking athletes exit the back of the circle.

CHECK-OFF LIST		Tick appropriate box		
		GOOD	FAIR	POOR
EQUIPMENT	Red flag for a foul attempt			
	White flag for a legal attempt			
	Record sheet			
	Pen			
	Tape measure			
	List of competitors			
	Correctly weighted shot for the age group			
	Cloths for drying shot in wet conditions			
PRE EVENT	Competitors muster in the correct place			
	Correct marked areas			
	Good condition of the shot put circle			
	Designated area for the competitors			
PRACTICAL EFFECTIVENESS				
JUDGE ONE	Watches for hand faults outside the circle on his side			
	Watches for foot faults – exiting from the front of the circle on his side of the circle			
	Calls up the competitors – Records the distances			
	Checks the equipment safely stored throughout the event			
JUDGE TWO	Watches for foot faults on top of the stopboard on his side			
	Watches for faults on the top of the circle on his side of the stopboard			
	Makes clear signals indicating a fair or foul attempt after put			
	One of the other judges takes the tape over the stopboard and past the centre of the circle			
	The other judge reads off the distance from the inner part of the stopboard			
JUDGE THREE	Stands out in the sector			
	Checks the shot lands within the arc			
	Places the spike at the end of the tape measure at the edge of the shot indentation (nearest the circle)			
	Keeps the measure steady			
POST EVENT	All attempts correctly recorded			
	Result announced			
	Result sent to the results table			
	Equipment left safely			

Signals for athletics – Shot put judge

When umpiring, judging or refereeing use of hand signals makes the decisions made clear to all those involved and watching. The signals are simple and easy to understand. The official is expected to make them clearly, confidently and as soon after the incident/attempt as possible.

Prior to the attempt.

Signal as a result of a successful attempt.

Signal as a result of an unsuccessful attempt.

Analysis of Performance for GCSE PE – Teacher Guide

Analysis of the Officials – Football referee

CHECK-OFF LIST		Tick appropriate box		
		GOOD	FAIR	POOR
EQUIPMENT	Notebook			
	Pencil			
	Discipline cards			
	Watch/stopwatch			
	Correct dress			
	Neutral coloured top			
	Spare pencil			
	Spare watch			
	Coin			
	Whistle attached to wrist. Spare whistle.			
PRE MATCH CHECK	Pitch			
	Corner flags			
	Goals and nets			
	No jewellery on players			
	Safe dress – boots/hair			
	Correct numbers on shirts			
	The correct number of players on pitch			
PRACTICAL EFFECTIVENESS	Responds quickly to the play			
	Clear use of whistle			
	Clear verbal instructions			
	Clear hand signals			
	Consistent decision making			
	Impartial treatment of teams			
	Correct position for – general play			
	corners			
	penalties			
	Works as a team with other officials			
	Record – score			
	disciplinary action			
	Keeps control of the game			
	Allows play to flow when appropriate			
	Keeps up with play			
POST MATCH	Announces final score			
	Writes match report and send off			

Signals for football referees

According to the laws of football the referee only has two **mandatory signals** to make:

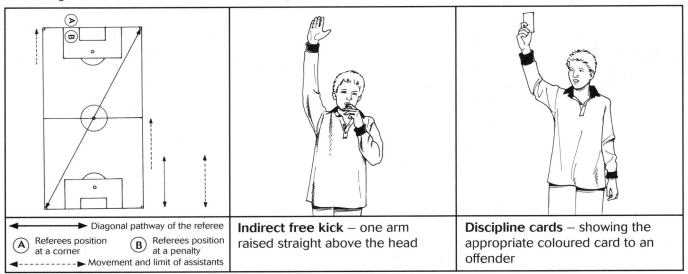

Diagonal pathway of the referee
(A) Referees position at a corner
(B) Referees position at a penalty
← - - - - → Movement and limit of assistants

Indirect free kick – one arm raised straight above the head

Discipline cards – showing the appropriate coloured card to an offender

There are various **approved signals** giving instructions to the players:

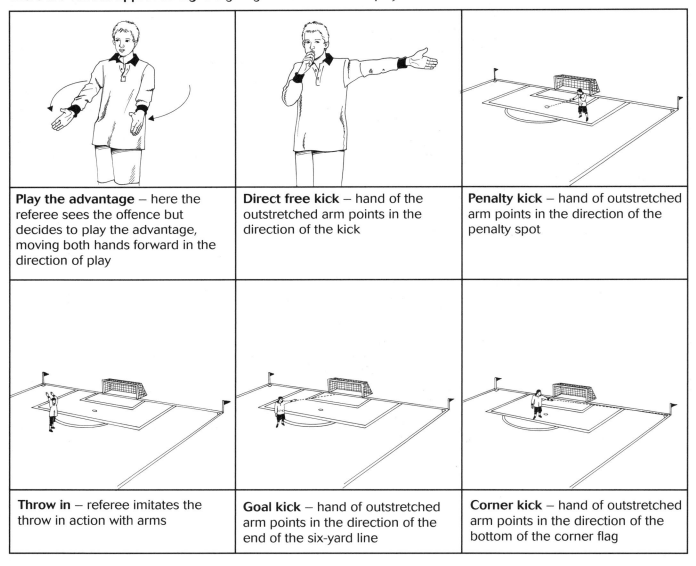

Play the advantage – here the referee sees the offence but decides to play the advantage, moving both hands forward in the direction of play

Direct free kick – hand of the outstretched arm points in the direction of the kick

Penalty kick – hand of outstretched arm points in the direction of the penalty spot

Throw in – referee imitates the throw in action with arms

Goal kick – hand of outstretched arm points in the direction of the end of the six-yard line

Corner kick – hand of outstretched arm points in the direction of the bottom of the corner flag

There are some **unofficial signals** used to inform the players of offences committed. These signals include:

Handling the ball – one hand touches the other

Pushing – both hands are in front of the body, with fingers up, and move in and out in a pushing motion

Analysis of the Officials – Netball umpire

CHECK-OFF LIST		Tick appropriate box		
		GOOD	FAIR	POOR
EQUIPMENT	Rules book			
	Scorecard			
	Pen			
	Discipline cards			
	Watch/stopwatch			
	Correct dress			
	Neutral coloured top			
PRE MATCH CHECK	Court for dangerous objects			
	Court surrounds for safety			
	Posts safety			
	Fingernail length of players			
	No jewellery worn by players			
	Hair tied back			
	Correct dress			
	Correct bibs			
	Players in correct position			
	No chewing gum			
PRACTICAL EFFECTIVENESS	Responds quickly to the play			
	Clear use of whistle			
	Clear verbal instructions			
	Clear and correct hand signals			
	Consistent decision making			
	Impartial treatment of teams			
	Correct court position – general play			
	– goal area play			
	Manages and controls game			
	Works as a team with other umpire			
	Records score/disciplinary action			
	Announces score and centre pass after goals			
POST MATCH	Announces final score			

Signals and movement of netball umpires

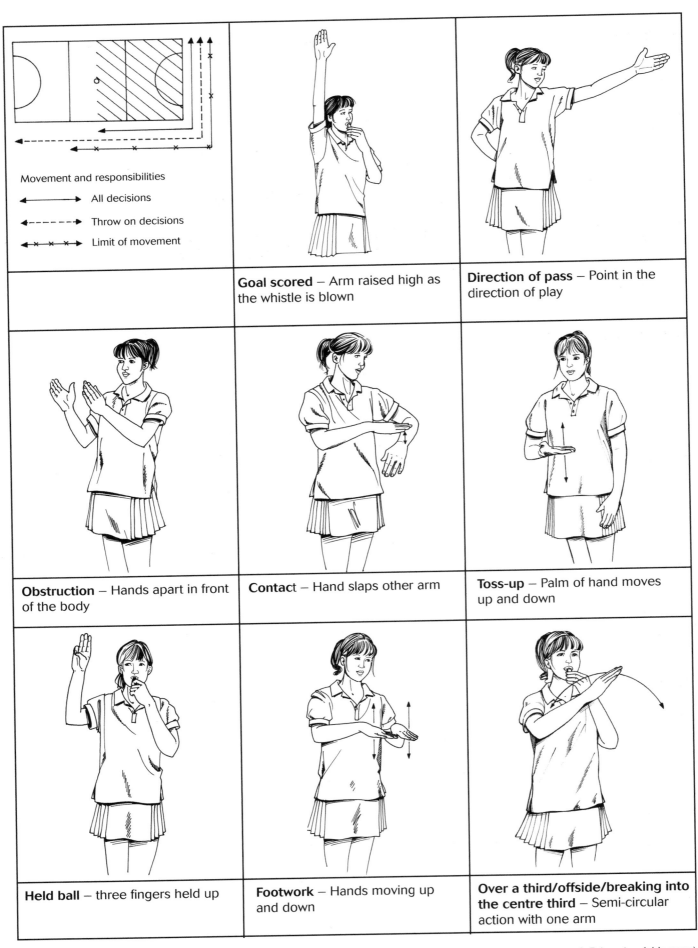

Movement and responsibilities

→← All decisions

←---→ Throw on decisions

←-x-x-x→ Limit of movement

Goal scored – Arm raised high as the whistle is blown

Direction of pass – Point in the direction of play

Obstruction – Hands apart in front of the body

Contact – Hand slaps other arm

Toss-up – Palm of hand moves up and down

Held ball – three fingers held up

Footwork – Hands moving up and down

Over a third/offside/breaking into the centre third – Semi-circular action with one arm

Terminology for Athletics

No throw

1 The performer touches the ground outside the circle in the action.

2 Exits from the front half of the circle after the throw.

3 Steps onto or over the kick board during the put (with any part of the body).

4 Releases the shot away from the neck.

5 Performer puts the shot outside the landing sector.

Weights of shot

Men

Under 13 – 3.25kg

Under 15 – 4kg

Under 17 – 5kg

Juniors – 6.25kg

Seniors – 7.26kg

Women

Under 13 – 2.72kg

Under 15 – 3.25kg

Under 17 – 4kg

Juniors – 4kg

Seniors – 4kg

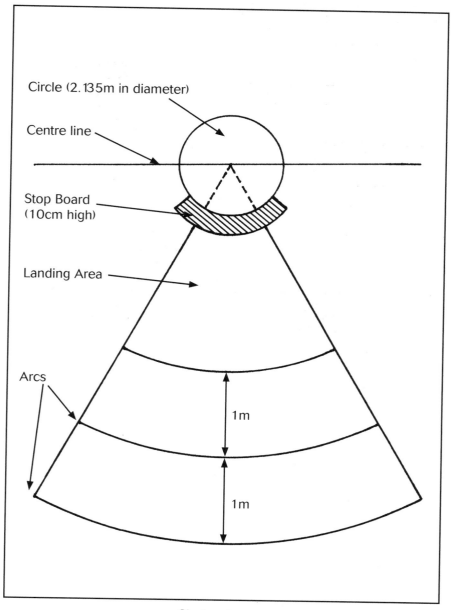

Shot put area

Safety

back support belt – stabilises the spine in the put action

throwing protocol – waiting to be invited to throw

carrying shot – if no carrying equipment then carry the shot in both hands at the front of the body

procedure at an event – stay in the competitors' area

warm up – warm up the whole body prior to the event and whilst waiting for your turn

Terminology for Football

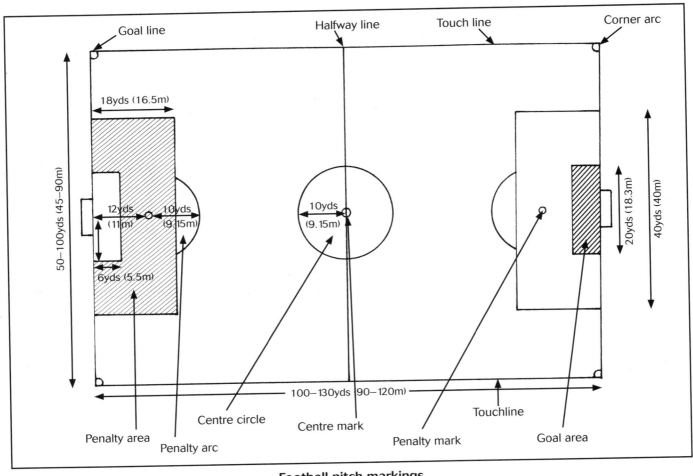

Football pitch markings

Additional time – added time at the end of the half due to stoppages and substitutions

Blind side – the side of the player out of vision line to a pass or a moving player

Centre/cross – the act of kicking the ball towards the penalty spot from the sidelines

Chip – playing the ball with backspin, into the air avoiding the opposition

Covering – taking up the position of a team-mate who commits himself to a tackle or move

Dead ball – when a ball is kicked from a stationary position

Defensive wall – a line of players between the goal and 10yds (9.15m) away from the placement of the ball at a free kick

Extra time – pre-determined time, usually two halves of fifteen minutes, played after the ninety minutes when the scores are level, to determine a winner

Killing the ball – when a player controls the ball to a dead stop

Marking – keeping close to an opponent making it difficult for him to get away or receive a pass

Offside – when an attacking player receives or runs for the ball, from a forward pass, with less than two defenders between them and the goal

Overlapping – when a player, usually a defensive player, runs past his team-mate, along the touchline, into an attacking position

Running off the ball – the movement of a player, without the ball, into a space to receive a pass or create space

Selling a dummy – faking a pass or direction of a dribble to outplay the opposition

Set piece – an organised and rehearsed play from a dead ball situation

Square pass – a pass played at right angles to the side line across the pitch

Through ball – a pass played between the defenders

Analysis of Performance for GCSE PE – Teacher Guide © Folens (copiable page)

Terminology for Netball

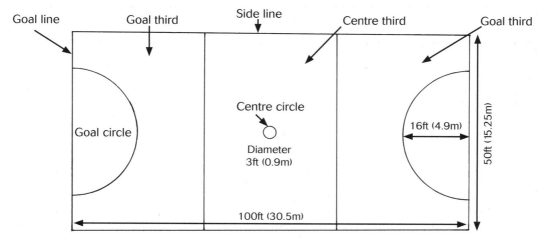

Dimensions of a netball court

Rule terminology

Infringements – When an infringement takes place the umpire will call the play in the following order:

1) **The infringement** – 'footwork blue centre';
2) **The penalty** – 'free pass';
3) **The team to take the penalty** – 'to reds'

Penalty pass – a pass given for contact, obstruction or intimidation where the offender is further penalised by having to stand by but slightly away from the player taking the pass

Contact – contacting a player or the ball held by the opponent – Penalty pass

Obstruction – marking the player with ball from less than three feet (0.9m), or marking a player without the ball stopping their progress with their arms or any other part of their body – Penalty pass

Intimidation – a player may not step late into the path of a runner or take landing space of a player in the air – the offence is treated as obstruction – Penalty pass

Free pass – a pass given for infringements such as footwork, offside, replaying the ball etc. The offender can be active during the awarded pass

Footwork – taking more than a land and step movement of the feet whilst in possession of the ball – Free pass

Over a third – the ball is thrown completely over one third without any player having possession i.e. a pass from a goal line throw in to a player in the centre third – Free pass

Held ball – a player is in possession of the ball for longer than 3 seconds – Free pass

Replayed ball – once a player has had control of the ball they may not lose and regain possession without a third party making contact with the ball – Free pass

Short pass – as the ball is passed there is no room for another player between the hands of the thrower and receiver – Free pass

Offside – during play a player encroaches into an area they are not allowed in – Free pass

Out of court – the ball or player in possession of the ball has touched the ground or object outside the court area – Throw on – equal to a free pass outside the court.

General terminology

Holding space – standing still on the court so movement takes the opposition by surprise

Feint and dodge – small movement made away from intended final space of ball reception followed by quick run into space

Running pass – catching, landing, stepping and throwing all in one action

Toss up – way of deciding a simultaneous foul by members of opposing teams – Players stand opposite

each other with hands by their sides – umpire tosses ball from a central position, up to the height of the smallest player's shoulders, as they blow the whistle

Man-to-man defence – each player takes sole responsibility of marking one player

Zone defence – players are responsible for defending a space rather than a player

Blocking – defensive ploy where the space three feet away from the opposition is taken up by defender, preventing the opposition using that space

Discuss findings with the performer sheet

After analysing a person's performance your conclusions of their strengths and weaknesses will be formulated. Relating these to the performer and inviting their opinion, as a two-way interaction, forms the feedback process. For the analysis to be useful it is important to share the findings with the performer. Discussing the contents of the analysis will help the performer to understand the improvements and changes needed for the future. The questions you ask should be easy to understand, relevant to the activity and make the performer think about their performance.

Examples of questions that can be used

Questions relating to training

Did the programme make you work hard?

Was the programme easy to complete?

Was the programme varied enough to keep your interest?

What areas of skill-related fitness did the programme concentrate on?

Did you get feedback after each session?

Were you tested before the programme started and after it was completed?

Did you think before you were tested that you were stronger than you actually were?

Which part of the programme was your favourite?

Who motivated you throughout the programme? (Self/Coach/Teacher/Friends)

What have you learnt by completing the programme?

How would you change the contents of the training if you were starting again?

What evidence have you kept relating to the programme's start and finish?

How do you think you have improved since the start of the training?

Questions relating to performance

How do you think you performed?

What were your strengths?

What were your weaknesses?

Did you think you put your training into operation?

What area of skills will you work on as a result of this performance?

What targets will you set yourself for the future?

Did the conditions affect your performance at all?

Did the refereeing help the game?

Were the opposition a good match for your skills?

Questions relating to team performance

How did you contribute to the team performance?

In which area of the pitch were you the most effective?

How did your side/area of the team perform as a small unit?

How effective were the team tactics?

Which team member was the strongest player today and why?

How did the team deal with the opponent's attacks?

Example Questionnaire

NAME	FORM	DATE

ACTIVITY

Please answer the questions in the spaces provided

PERSONAL ABILITY

1 What do you think is your main strength in the activity?

_____

2 What do you think is your main weakness in the activity?

_____

3 In the activity, which skill did you find the most difficult to perform?

_____

TRAINING PROGRAMME

4 Did the training programme devised for you suit your ability?

_____

5 What personal qualities did it take to complete the training programme?

_____

6 Are there any changes, from your experience, you would make to a future training programme?

_____

7 Which area did the training programme improve most?

_____

FEEDBACK

8 What kinds of feedback did you receive on your performance?

_____

9 Was the feedback given clear?

_____

10 How did you react to being given feedback on your performance?

_____

11 Was the feedback relevant to your performance?

_____

OVERALL REACTION

12 How has your understanding changed on the effectiveness of using a training programme?

_____

13 Does your play differ in any way from that before the training programme?

_____

14 What is the most significant thing you have learnt from completing the training programme?

_____

THANK YOU FOR COMPLETING THIS QUESTIONNAIRE

Example of a Five-point scale feedback sheet

Five-point scale feedback sheet

CANDIDATE	ACTIVITY/POSITION	DATE

Read the questions carefully.
Tick the most appropriate box (5 is the most positive, 1 the most negative)

		5	4	3	2	1
PERSONAL ABILITY						
1	How well did you perform when defending?					
2	How well did you perform when attacking?					
3	How successful was your long passing?					
4	How successful was your short passing?					
5	How effective was your tackling?					
6	To what level did you contribute to the team tactics?					
7	Weakest skill .... How effective was it in competition?					
8	Strongest skill .... How effective was it in competition?					
9	How competitive were you?					
10	Did the conditions affect your performance?					
TRAINING PROGRAMME						
11	How much did the training programme suit your ability?					
12	How determined were you to complete the training as well as you could?					
13	Name your favourite part of the programme .... How much did it positively affect your performance?					
14	How much is your strength improved?					
15	How much is your stamina improved?					
16	How much are your skills improved?					
FEEDBACK						
17	How helpful was the feedback you were given?					
18	How accurate did you think the feedback was?					
19	How detailed was the feedback given?					
20	How varied was the feedback given?					
21	How clear was the feedback given?					
22	How positive were your reactions to the feedback?					
23	How relevant was the feedback to your performance?					
OVERALL REACTION						
24	How has your understanding changed on the effectiveness of using a training programme?					
25	Does your play differ in any way from that before the training programme?					
26	What is the most significant thing you have learnt from completing the training programme?					

AQA analysis form

Candidate	Date	Analysis attempt	Own/others' performance		
Activity	Playing position	Experience	Playing conditions		
Analysis of performance	Comments				
1. Strength 1					
2. Strength 2					
3. Weakness 1					
4. Weakness 2					
Skill-related fitness needed	Understanding the activity				
Improving performance	Nature/cause of strength/weakness				
1.					
2.					
3.					
4.					

AQA analysis form (side 2)

Targets for progress		Measuring		Monitoring

Corrective measures	Practice set up

Analysis of Performance for GCSE PE – Teacher Guide © Folens (copiable page)

Edexcel analysis form

Candidate		Date		Analysis attempt	
Activity	**Playing position**		**Experience**	**Conditions**	

Observation

Live game

Live practice

Video

Photo

Time lapsed photo

Analysis – Important components of health/skill-related fitness

Understand the action of a perfect model	**Evaluation**

Rule infringements

Edexcel analysis form *(side 2)*

Planning for improvement – Components of skill-related fitness to improve

Training principles to apply

Practices to help improvement (isolating part of the action)

Tactics to aid improvement

OCR analysis form

Candidate	Date	Analysis attempt	Own/others' performance
Activity	Playing position	Experience	Playing conditions

Identified skills needed for the activity –

Strengths in the performance

1

2

To improve strengths

1 Training principles

Methods

Practices

- -

2 Training principles

Methods

Practices

OCR analysis form *(side 2)*

Weaknesses in the performance	Reasons for the weaknesses
1	
2	
3	

How to correct the weaknesses

1 Training principles

Methods

Practices

2 Training principles

Methods

Practices

3 Training principles

Methods

Practices

Record of discussions on findings

Analysis of Performance for GCSE PE – Teacher Guide © Folens (copiable page)

A check-off list

Analysis sheet for –		Tick if successful

Officiating sheet

Tick appropriate box	Good	Fair	Poor
EQUIPMENT			
PRE MATCH			
PRACTICAL EFFECTIVENESS			
POST MATCH			

Training matrix

	RECORD OF COMPLETED TESTING AND EXERCISE SESSIONS					
	Name		**Date**		**Activity training for**	
	Test results					
Test For						
Test Type						
W E E K 1						

TRAINING SESSIONS TO COMPLETE *(Tick box if completed)*

W E E K 2	☐	☐	☐	☐
W E E K 3	☐	☐	☐	☐
W E E K 4	☐	☐	☐	☐
W E E K 5	☐	☐	☐	☐

RETEST RESULTS

W E E K 6	**R E S U L T**						
	C H A N G E S						

Football Performance Sheet

FOOTBALL PERFORMANCE SHEET			
Candidate	Position	Conditions	Date

OUTFIELD PLAYER *(Tick or cross depending on success)*		GOALKEEPER *(Tick or cross depending on success)*	
PASSING –		**SHOTS SAVED –**	
Short		One-handed to left	
Medium		One-handed to right	
Long		Two-handed to left	
Shot on Goal		Two-handed to right	
Header		**CONTROL –**	
Throw in		High Catch	
BALL CONTROL –		**CLEARANCES –**	
1 Touch		One-handed Punch	
2 Touches		Two-handed Punch	
Dribbling		Kick	
Chesting Down		Header	
Control on Thigh			
GENERAL –		**PASSES –**	
Tackles		Underarm	
Fouls		Overarm	

Analysis of Performance for GCSE PE – Teacher Guide © Folens (copiable page)

Netball Performance Sheet

NETBALL PERFORMANCE SHEET			
Candidate	**Assessed position**	**Playing conditions**	**Date**

SKILLS *(Tick or cross depending on success)*		INFRINGEMENT *(Tick or cross depending on success)*	
PASSING –		**CONTACT –**	
Chest		Obstruction	
Javelin		Footwork	
Bounce		Offside	
Two-handed overhead		Replayed ball	
Throw on		Held ball	
DEFENDING –		Over a third	
Interception		**SHOOTING** *(Put a cross in position of shot)* Record the number of successful shots for each area	
Blocking			
GENERAL –		**NEAR**	
Toss up		**MID**	
		FAR	

Useful addresses and websites

Football
'The Soccer Referee's Manual' second edition
David Ager
A&C Black
ISBN 0 7136 4925 9

Netball
The All England Netball Association Limited
Netball House
9 Paynes Park
Hitchin
Hertfordshire
SG5 1EH
www.england-netball.co.uk

Basketball
England Basketball
England Institute of Sport – Sheffield
Coleridge Road
Sheffield
S9 5DA
www.englandbasketball.co.uk

Rounders
National Rounders Association
3 Denehurst Avenue
Nottingham
NE8 5DA

Cricket
'The Laws of Cricket' The National Cricket Association
Headquarters
Lord's Cricket ground
London
NW8 8QZ

Tennis
'LTA Tennis Rules Book' Coaching Department
The LTA Trust
The Queen's Club
West Kensington
London
W14 9EG

Athletics
'Rules for Competition' UK Athletics
Athletics House
10 Harborne Road
Edgbaston
Birmingham
B15 3AA
ISBN 0 85134 149 7
www.ukathletics.net

UK Sport
40 Bernard Street
London
WC1N 1ST
info@uksport.gov.uk

Analysis of Performance for GCSE PE – Teacher Guide

Analysis of Performance for GCSE PE – Teacher Guide

Analysis of Performance for GCSE PE – Teacher Guide